Stage 15

Non-Fiction
Teaching Notes

Andrew Hammond

OXFORD

UNIVERSITY PRESS

Contents

Introduction

TreeTops Non-Fiction is an exciting extension to the *TreeTops* range. All the titles have been chosen to appeal to 7–11 year olds and have an appropriate reading ability level at their particular Stage. *TreeTops* Stages follow on from the *Oxford Reading Tree* Stages, and are designed to be used flexibly with your individual pupil's reading ability. The levelling guide on page 5 gives you an indication of how the Stages correspond to the Year and age of the average pupil, together with the relevant match from the National Curriculum Level or Scottish, Northern Irish and Welsh equivalents.

Each book includes a Contents page, an Index and/or a Glossary of specialist terms or equivalent. These features enable teachers to develop children's information retrieval skills. In addition features of non-fiction texts, such as sub-headings, text boxes, and captions help children learn to skim read a text for information. The series aims to fascinate children with surprising and interesting information.

How to introduce the books

Before reading the book, always read the title and talk about the possible content. Encourage the children to articulate what they already know about the subject, what they would like to find out and how they will use this book to do it. Complete the reading session with the pupils telling you what they have learned.

This booklet provides suggestions for using the book with groups of pupils or individuals. Suggestions are also provided for speaking and listening, further reading activities, ICT links and writing. These may be used as a follow on to the reading or used at another time.

Guided Reading Cards with built-in comprehension are available for each book. These provide detailed guidance for using the book for guided reading. Parental notes are included with each individual book.

Cross-curricular links with QCA/NLS objectives

Title	QCA Cross-curricular links	NLS objectives
Robot – Friend or Foe?	Design and Technology: 6D Controllable vehicles	Y6 T1 T13 secure understanding of the features of non-chronological reports Y6 T2 T16 identify the features of balanced written arguments Y6 T2 T19 write a balanced report of a controversial issue
What's Left Behind?	History 10 What can we find out about ancient Egypt from what has survived? 16 How can we find out about the Indus Valley civilisation?	Y6 T1 T16 to use the styles and conventions of journalism to report on, e.g. real or imagined events Y6 T1 T17 to write non-chronological reports linked to other subjects
Pirates	History 19 What were the effects of Tudor exploration? 6C A Viking case study	Y6 T1 T11 distinguish between biography and autobiography: distinguishing between fact, opinion and fiction Y6 T2 T10 to use different genres as models to write, e.g. short extracts, sequels, additional episodes, alternative endings
Eyes of Every Shape and Size	Science 6F How we see things	Y6 T1 T13 to secure understanding of the features of non-chronological reports Y6 T1 T17 to write non-chronological reports linked to other subjects
Michael Rosen's Scrapbook	History 20 What can we learn about recent history from studying the life of a famous person?	Y6 T1 T11 to distinguish between biography and autobiography Y6 T2 T5 to analyse how messages, moods, feelings and attitudes are conveyed in poetry Y6 T2 T9 to increase familiarity with significant poets and writers of the past
Reach for the Skies	Citizenship 1 Taking part 5 Living in a diverse world	Y6 T1 T11 to distinguish between biography and autobiography Y6 T1 T14 to develop the skills of biographical and autobiographical writing in role, adopting distinctive voices, e.g. historical characters

Levels Chart

Title	TreeTops Stage 15	England NC level	Scotland	Northern Ireland	Wales
Robot – Friend or Foe?	Year 6 Terms 1 and 2 Ages 10–11	Level 4/5	Level D/E	**Reading Activities:** b, f, g, h Outcomes: e, f, g, k	**Reading:** Range: 1, 3, 4 Skills: 6, 7, 8 Language development: 1, 2
What's Left Behind?	Year 6 Term 1 Ages 10–11	Level 4/5	Level D/E	**Writing** Opportunities: b, c Outcomes: b, c, d	**Writing:** Range: 1, 4 Skills: 2, 3, 8 Language development: 1, 2, 4
Pirates	Year 6 Terms 1 and 2 Ages 10–11	Level 4/5	Level D/E		
Eyes of Every Shape and Size	Year 6 Term 1 Ages 10–11	Level 4/5	Level D/E		
Michael Rosen's Scrapbook	Year 6 Terms 1 and 2 Ages 10–11	Level 4/5	Level D/E		
Reach for the Skies	Year 6 Term 1 Ages 10–11	Level 4/5	Level D/E		

Robot – Friend or Foe?

Reading the book with individuals or guided reading groups

Introducing the book

- Look at the front cover together in class. Invite the children to consider whether this book will be fiction or non-fiction writing. How do they know?
- Focus on the use of a question in the main title. Discuss the terms 'friend' and 'foe'. Ask: *What does a question like this suggest about the type of text it might be?* Encourage the children to flick through the pages and note the repeated use of questions throughout.
- Introduce or revisit the term 'discussion text', in which information is provided, two sides of an issue are presented and readers are prompted to formulate and discuss opinions of their own in response.
- Ask the children to consider some of the features of a discussion text.

Strategy check

- Explain that this text may contain several new words and phrases. Discuss ways in which readers can come to understand the meanings of these words – by using the Glossary and/or by reading around words to decipher meaning through context.
- Model this process by choosing two unfamiliar words, looking one up in the Glossary at the back and then using textual cues for the other.

Focus of reading

- As they read through the book, encourage the children to differentiate between fact and opinion, and to form their own views in response to what they read.
- Remind the children of the frequent use of questions to provoke debate about the role of robots.

Independent reading

- Observe the children as they read the text, checking particularly that they are able to identify and respond to the 'What do you think?' boxes.
- Check that the pupils are pausing to take note of definitions and explanations when they appear within the text, and referring to the Glossary when necessary.

Return and respond to the text

- Ask the children to re-read the book and identify (and note down) situations when robots perform tasks that lie beyond human capabilities (e.g. exploring the solar system).
- Ask the children to repeat the above exercise, only this time looking for situations where a robot is carrying out a task usually done by humans (e.g. serving a meal).
- Invite the children to find out where the term 'robot' comes from and to identify early forms and uses of robots. They may refer to the Contents page to guide their research.

Further reading activities

- Ask the children to flick through the book and find examples of the language features found in a non-chronological report, including: headings, paragraphs, illustrations, captions, annotations and word banks.

- Ask the children to consider how robots enable us to make scientific breakthroughs – to find new solutions to old problems.

Speaking and listening activities

- Working in pairs, ask the children to debate the value of robots, one partner in favour of letting robots do more for us, the other wary of how dependent we have become on robots.
- Hold a class debate in which the following motion is proposed: 'This House believes that the more robots do for us, the more primitive we become'.

ICT links

- Invite the children to use a combination of ICT and manual skills to design their own robots, annotating them to show the main components (as featured on pages 10 and 11).

- Research further information on robots at:
  www.realrobots.co.uk
  www.active-robots.com
  www.channel4.com/science/microsites/R/robots

Writing

- Discuss the layout and language features of a balanced discussion text using the book as a model, e.g. words and devices to distinguish between views, and between fact and opinion; use of questions to prompt discussion; present tense; third person.
- Ask the children to plan and draft their own discussion text presenting the advantages and disadvantages of using robots. They may include a short editorial at the end in which they judge whether a robot is a 'friend or foe'.

What's Left Behind?

Reading the book with individuals or guided reading groups

Introducing the book

- Look together at the front cover; discuss the title. Invite the children to consider what this book might be about – the text type and subject.
- Read through the Contents together. Ask: *Do the headings give us clues to the text type? Which one is the instruction text? How can we tell?*
- Discuss the features of non-chronological texts, including: headings, captions, annotations, glossary, photographs and diagrams.
- Ask the children to consider, as they read through the book, how decisions have been made about page layout and design to enable effective and efficient reading.

Strategy check

- Model how to use the Glossary by first reading the paragraph at the bottom of page 4 and focusing on the word 'artefacts', and then looking the word up in the Glossary on page 31.
- Discuss with the children the importance of being able to skim and scan text to retrieve information effectively and efficiently.

Focus of reading

- Pose this key question to the children: *How can we find out what has happened in the past?* and invite them to keep this in mind throughout their reading of the book. Ask the children to keep a record of how and where historical clues can be found.

Independent reading

- Encourage the children to pause at intervals throughout the book to consider rhetorical questions asked in the text to make the reader think deeply about the issue, e.g. 'Why were the cities abandoned?' on page 9.
- Remind the children that words presented in bold type can be found in the Glossary. Ensure that children are using this feature. You may wish to encourage them to begin their own word bank – for use in future writing projects.

Return and respond to the text

- Ask the children to begin compiling a list of comprehension questions that may be used to guide others' reading of the book. As they flick through the pages, invite them to pose questions about the topics, themes and facts – the answers to which lie within the text or artwork.
- Ask the children to name, and explain, three fascinating facts they have learned from reading this book.
- Invite the children to appraise the text by evaluating its double-page spreads, in terms of layout, design, ease of reading and understanding. *Which pages are the most effective? Why?*

Further reading activities

- Ask the children to work in pairs. Their task is to think about, and discuss together, how historical research lies beyond books. *How can we use our senses to unearth the past? What can we do to find clues around us?*
- Ask the children to read pages 20–21. Invite them to explain how we know that this is an instruction text, by identifying its features.

Speaking and listening activities

● Working in pairs, ask the children to turn to pages 20–21, and read through the instructions.
● Invite the children to imagine they are presenters on a DIY television programme. The subject is... 'How to Mummify a Body'.
● Working together, the children will need to decide how to turn the text into a chronological sequence of oral instructions to accompany a demonstration.

ICT links

● Ask the children to use IT skills to turn their draft notes into a publishable format.

● Invite the children to choose a particular topic from the book and research it further, drawing on a range of multimedia resources including: Internet websites, information books, encyclopaedias, television documentaries and posters.

Writing

● Ask the children to look at pages 22–23. Discuss the archaeological find known as 'Lindow Man'.
● Ask the children to design a newspaper article in which the news of this amazing discovery is first reported. They will need to focus on the facts presented in the book – and to expand on these by adding fictional eyewitness statements and experts' advice.

Pirates

Reading the book with individuals or guided reading groups

Introducing the book

- Consider the book's title and front cover. Invite the children to suggest the genre for the book. Ask: *Does it look more like fiction than other titles in the series?*
- Glance at the Contents page together and review thinking.
- Consider why the theme of pirates is still as exciting today as ever. Invite the children to explain why pirates appeal to them.
- Brainstorm (using a mind-map on the board) the words and phrases the children expect to find in this book – those synonymous with pirates, e.g. treasure, pieces of eight, Long John Silver, high seas, buccaneers.

Strategy check

- Explain that the children may find other words and phrases in this book that are less familiar to them. Ask them how they will find out what they mean. (Look for clues in the word, read around the text, look for clarifications, use the Glossary.)
- Remind the children of the mind-map from the Introduction. Choose one phrase (Long John Silver) and ask the children how we can find out if it is mentioned in the book. (*We use an Index.*) Refer to page 32.

Focus of reading

- Explain to the children that the main aims for this unit will be to practise and extend their skills in skimming and scanning texts to retrieve key information.
- Encourage the pupils to make good use of headings, captions, paragraphs, labels and illustrations when seeking information in answer to key questions set (see below).

Independent reading

- As the children read through the text, check that they are focusing their reading to respond to specific questions – taking their cues from the Contents, Index and Glossary.
- Invite the children to consider the difference between historical evidence and anecdotal evidence (eyewitness accounts featured in the Witness boxes throughout).

Return and respond to the text

- Set the pupils a number of key questions to guide their reading, e.g. *What does Julius Caesar have to do with the theme of pirates? What happened on the island of Lindisfarne in AD 793? Why was it better to be a Privateer than a Pirate?*
- Based on what they have read, ask the children to consider the character traits of a typical pirate. *What sort of person would he/she be?* Pages 22–25 will be of particular help here.

Further reading activities

- Encourage the children to set their own questions based on other sections of the book.
- Then ask the children to find a partner to exchange their comprehension questions.

Speaking and listening activities

- In pairs, ask the children to work through the 'Are you a pirate or a victim?' quiz on page 30 together and then discuss how the words 'pirate' and 'piracy' have evolved.

- Read pages 6 and 7 again. Explain to the children the following task: to work in groups, producing a two-minute dramatic sketch in which they act out the story of how the townsfolk of Dublin beat the Vikings in AD 1171.

ICT links

- Read pages 22 and 23 together. Ask the children to create their own 'Wanted!' posters which focus on one of the pirates featured. They will need to think about: name, appearance, character, crimes committed, reward.

- Read page 15. Ask the children to write a job advertisement for the post of Chief Buccaneer. Discuss the purpose, layout and features of a job advertisement.

Writing

- Ask the children to write a story entitled *Caesar's Revenge* in which Caesar hunts down the pirates who once captured him and brings them to 'justice'.
- You will need to revisit pages 4 and 5 and help the pupils to plan the scenes for this story, beginning with Caesar chartering the fleet of ships.
- Think about: first/third person narrative, the plot and the description of the setting.

Eyes of Every Shape and Size

Reading the book with individuals or guided reading groups

Introducing the book

- Look together at the cover. Invite the children to suggest what sort of text this might be – fiction or non-fiction, explanatory/informative/discursive, etc.
- Encourage the children to share any interesting facts they know about eyes. Will they find these facts in this book?
- Invite the pupils to think of questions they would like answered about eyes. For example, How do they work? Which creature has the largest eyes? Or the most eyes? Record the questions on the board.
- Read the Introduction together. Discuss what the purpose of this text might be.

Strategy check

- Remind the children of the strategies they may use when they come across unfamiliar words, e.g. bold words can be found in the Glossary; reading around the word to infer sense and meaning; looking up words in dictionaries.

Focus of reading

- Explain that the objective of the session is to ascertain the layout and language features of explanatory texts (as opposed to non-chronological reports), so that they may write their own on a similar theme.
- They will begin by reading, discussing and modelling the text on page 7 (beginning: 'At the front of the eye...').

Independent reading

- Encourage the children to recognise when they are reading a non-chronological report or an explanatory text, and to be aware of the author's intentions when writing a particular paragraph (i.e. to inform or to explain).
- Observe the strategies the children use when encountering difficult words and phrases. Praise those that refer to the Glossary or read around a word to infer meaning and sense.

Return and respond to the text

- Turn to page 7. Read out the paragraph together beginning 'At the front of the eye...' Explain to the children that this is a good example of an explanatory text. As such it moves beyond informing readers of interesting facts (like a non-chronological report) and actually explains how our eyes work.
- Discuss the language features of this text, including: subject specific terminology (shown in italics); words to show cause and effect; present tense and third person used throughout.
- Encourage the pupils to search for more explanatory texts within the book (good examples can be found on pages 8, 15, 21 and 28–29).

Further reading activities

- Revisit pages 18–19. Consider the design and content of these pages (in preparation for writing their own report text).
- In addition, the children could research other animal eyes not in the book and classify them according to their type.

Speaking and listening activities

● Invite the children to take turns in speaking for one minute beginning with the line: 'If I could have any eyes, I would have the eyes of a ...' Encourage them to give reasons for their choices.

● Ask the children to work in pairs. You will need plain paper and pencils. One partner (blindfolded) must follow the other's instructions for drawing a shape on a piece of paper – e.g. a house, car, flower.

ICT links

● Ask the children to use IT to produce their own 'Did you know?' fact file on the subject of eyes. They will need to present their fascinating facts in an exciting and eye-catching way, thinking about design, font size and type, colour and artwork.

● Invite the children to find out more about eyes by using the Internet.

Writing

● Ask the children to write an explanatory text, based on one of the examples in the book. They may choose the same subject, but must try to use their own words. Discuss the purpose, layout and language features of this text type first.

● Ask the children to represent the information on pages 18–19 in their own report text. They may use artwork, headings, captions and annotations.

Michael Rosen's Scrapbook

Reading the book with individuals or guided reading groups

Introducing the book

- Look together at the front cover. Ask the children to suggest what sort of book this is.
- Discuss the term 'scrapbook'. Ask: *What do we normally put in a scrapbook? How might we choose to record our memories?* (In photos and written recounts.)
- Explain that the book contains personal recounts, or autobiographical texts, some of which are written in poetic form.
- Invite the children to look at the Contents page and note how the headings confirm this, i.e. they sound like poem titles.

Strategy check

- This is a book about Michael Rosen's memories of childhood. As such, it is unlikely to contain too many unfamiliar or difficult words (it has no Glossary section). However, what it may have is a number of different names – of the people and places the author has encountered.
- Encourage the children to take note of these names – because some of them crop up in different poems.

Focus of reading

- Explain to the children that in many of the pages of this book, Michael recounts his childhood memories in the present tense, as if it is happening now (in the poems) and in the past tense, looking back (in the surrounding annotations). *How old is he in the poems/in the annotations?*
- Invite the children to consider the difference in tone between these two styles of narration. Focus on the different language features in each.

Independent reading

- Observe the children as they read through the text, highlighting the common features of personal recount (or autobiographical) text, including: personal pronouns; possessive adjectives; author's own thoughts and feelings.
- Encourage the children to see, as they read on, that the author gradually offers advice on how he writes his poems. The personal recounts become explanatory, informative style texts. Can the children see the difference?

Return and respond to the text

- Ask the children to consider Michael's childhood memories. *Are his poems realistic? Has he captured the essence of being young? Has he been able to see the world through young eyes again?*
- Encourage the children to consider how the author has used language (in the poems and in the annotations) to tell his story as vividly as possible.
- Invite the children, in pairs, to read through the text, and to find moments when the author's words remind them of their own experiences. The children may then share their own memories with one another.

Further reading activities

- Ask the children to work in pairs again and to take turns in reading one of Michael Rosen's poems aloud, bearing in mind the advice the author offers about how to read and understand his words.
- Where there is dialogue between characters in the poems, encourage the children to act out the conversations together. Invite volunteers to perform these to the rest of the class.

- Turn to pages 26–29. Explain that this is a good example of a chronological recount (or autobiographical) text. Highlight the use of time connectives and other devices to show progression (e.g. 'when', 'meanwhile', 'then').

Speaking and listening activities

- Hold a class discussion in which the effectiveness of the commentary throughout the book is assessed. *Was it useful?* Did it feel like they had Michael in the room, chatting to them as they read his poems?

ICT links

- Ask the children to use IT to produce a timeline showing the events in Michael Rosen's life as listed on pages 26–29.

- Find out more about Michael Rosen by visiting his website at www.michaelrosen.co.uk

Writing

- Ask the children to begin their own autobiographical text, using pages 26–29 as a model.
- Before beginning this process, invite the children to map out main events on a timeline, showing dates and names, etc.
- Revisit the common features of recount text together.

Reach for the Skies

Reading the book with individuals or guided reading groups

Introducing the book

- Look together at the front cover and read the title. Invite the children to suggest what the book might be about. *Will it be fiction or non-fiction?*
- Read the Contents page together. Are the pupils surprised? Were they expecting a science fiction story? *What do the headings on the Contents page suggest?*
- Explain to the children that this book looks at how people have conquered debilitating conditions to become successful in their own fields of expertise. It contains a series of mini-biographies and 'persuasive' information texts.
- Discuss the differences between biographical and autobiographical text.

Strategy check

- Read pages 4–5 together. Ask the children to suggest why the words 'conditions' and 'asthma' are in bold print.
- Turn to the Glossary of conditions (page 28) and the main Glossary (page 31) and discuss. Invite the children to find out the meanings of the two words in bold print on page 4. Analyse why one should be in the Glossary of conditions and the other in the main Glossary.
- Remind pupils that clues to the meaning of a word may lie in the sentences that surround it.

Focus of reading

- Explain that you want the children to consider, as they read the book, the type of text they are reading and the language features specific to the text type.
- Ask them to consider how the featured articles have motivating qualities to them – how and why should learning about the lives of others motivate and inspire readers?

Independent reading

- Observe the strategies the children use as they read through the book. Offer prompts where needed and provide clarification/advice where appropriate.
- Praise pupils when they look up difficult words in the Glossaries. Pause and question which Glossary a particular word in bold print may be found in. *How can we tell?*

Return and respond to the text

- Ask the children to read through the text and compile a list of common characteristics that the persons featured might share, i.e. What are the qualities one needs to beat adversity?
- Ask the children to compile a list of questions about the people in the book, to test other children's comprehension of the text.

Further reading activities

- Ask the children to consider which parts of the text are fact and which are opinion. Highlight how the timelines include facts, but lack the subject's views, thoughts and beliefs. *Are these important?*

- Ask the children to consider those people who they may have already known, but did not know suffered from a condition (e.g. Churchill suffering from dyslexia). Do they regard the person differently now? Do they admire them more or less?

Speaking and listening activities

- Ask the children to consider which person they most admire and why. Encourage them to articulate their views to a partner or within a class discussion.
- Working in pairs, ask the children to choose one famous person in the book and to conduct a 'radio interview' in which the presenter asks the special guest questions about his or her extraordinary life.

ICT links

- Ask the children to choose one person in the text who does not have a timeline and to use IT to construct one for them, using written evidence from the text, and extracting facts to display in a chronological diagram.
- The children could find out more about their famous person using Internet search engines to locate websites that feature them.

Writing

- Ask the children to choose one person in the book and to write, in role, an excerpt from their imaginary autobiographical diary. They may choose a particular day, or days, when their character faced a particularly difficult challenge and overcame it. Information may be gleaned from the text and from IT sources referred to above.

- Invite the children to write a newspaper article to appear in a Sunday newspaper, entitled 'Beating the Odds' in which they feature several people from the book sharing their stories and listing the characteristics they share.

Links to other TreeTops and OUP titles

Oxford Literacy Web Non-fiction KS2
TreeTops True Stories Stages 15–16
Oxford Connections

TreeTops Non-fiction Stage 15	*TreeTops* and OUP titles with similar subjects/themes
Robot – Friend or foe?	
What's Left Behind?	*TreeTops* Non-fiction *Wonderful Things* Oxford Connections *The Greeks* Web Weavers *Explorers and Discoveries* *TreeTops* True Stories *Tomb Raiders*
Pirates	*TreeTops* True *Stories Blackbeard's Last Stand*
Eyes of Every Shape and Size	Oxford Connections *Interdependence and Adaptation*
Michael Rosen's Scrapbook	KS2 Poetry Box
Reach for the Skies	

OXFORD
UNIVERSITY PRESS

Great Clarendon Street, Oxford OX2 6DP

Oxford University Press is a department of the University of Oxford. It furthers the University's objective of excellence in research, scholarship, and education by publishing worldwide in

Oxford New York

Auckland Cape Town Dar es Salaam Hong Kong Karachi
Kuala Lumpur Madrid Melbourne Mexico City Nairobi
New Delhi Shanghai Taipei Toronto

With offices in

Argentina Austria Brazil Chile Czech Republic France Greece
Guatemala Hungary Italy Japan Poland Portugal Singapore
South Korea Switzerland Thailand Turkey Ukraine Vietnam
Oxford is a registered trade mark of Oxford University Press
in the UK and in certain other countries

© Oxford University Press 2006

The moral rights of the author have been asserted

Database right Oxford University Press (maker)

First published 2005

British Library Cataloguing in Publication Data

Data available

ISBN 978-0-19-917943-5

10 9 8 7 6 5

Page make-up by Fakenham Photosetting Ltd, Fakenham, Norfolk

Printed in China by Imago

Paper used in the production of this book is a natural, recyclable product made from wood grown in sustainable forests. The manufacturing process conforms to the environmental regulations of the country of origin.